USBORNE
BEGINNER'S KNOWLEDGE

RAILWAYS & TRAINS

Caroline Young

Illustrated by Colin King

Designed by John Barker

Consultant: Mark Hambly and colleagues (Llangollen Railway Society)

With thanks to D. Mosley (National Railway Museum, York)

Contents

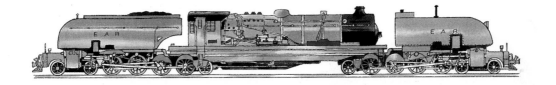

All about trains

This book tells the story of railways and the trains that run on them. It shows you how trains have changed from the first steam engines to the high speed trains of today.

The story of trains

Here are some of the trains you can find out about in this book. They do not all work in the same way but they all do the same job.

◄ **This is the first moving steam engine, or locomotive. It first ran in 1804.**

This is the ► *Rocket*. All steam locomotives built after it worked in the same basic way.

By the middle of ► the 1800s many steam locomotives in Europe looked like this.

This is one of the most famous steam locomotives ever. It is called *Flying Scotsman*. ▼

◄**This is a North American steam locomotive. It was built in 1850.**

What railways do

Before railways were built, many places were difficult to get to. The roads were bumpy and journeys were slow.

On the railways, more people could travel around. Trains could carry much more than a horse and carriage.

Trains carry large amounts of goods. They are often faster than trucks and can carry much more, as well.

Speed, smoke and noise

  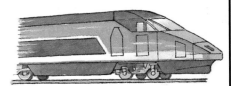

The first trains used the power of steam to make them move. They burned coal or wood as fuel and made steam, smoke and sparks as they went.

Diesel trains burn diesel oil. This sends power to an electric generator which makes the wheels turn. They can be smoky and noisy.

Electric trains use electricity. They do not need to carry their fuel. They can go faster than other trains and make little smoke or noise.

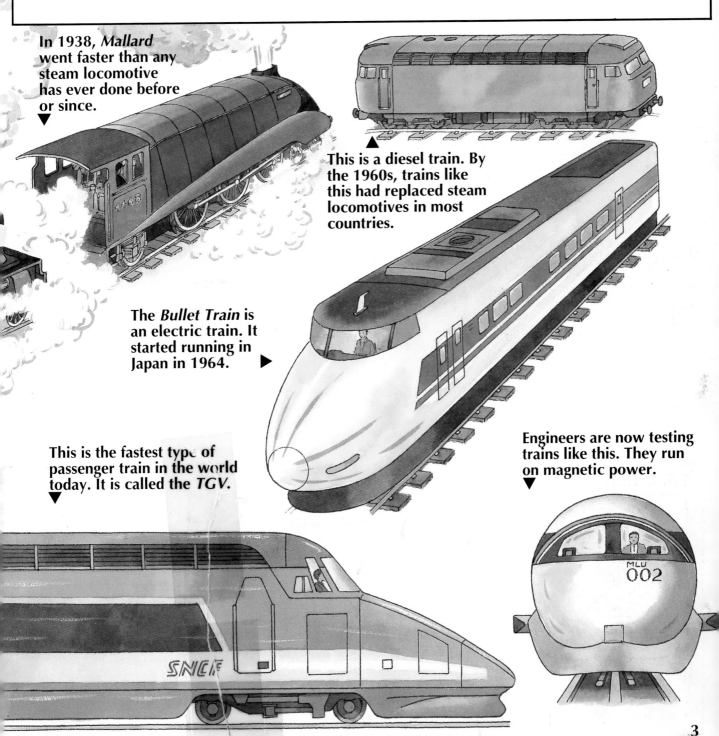

In 1938, *Mallard* went faster than any steam locomotive has ever done before or since.
▼

This is a diesel train. By the 1960s, trains like this had replaced steam locomotives in most countries.

The *Bullet Train* is an electric train. It started running in Japan in 1964. ▶

Engineers are now testing trains like this. They run on magnetic power.
▼

This is the fastest type of passenger train in the world today. It is called the *TGV*.
▼

Before the railways

Before the railways, it was difficult to travel from place to place. Traders found it slow and expensive to get their goods to where they were needed. People wanted a fast, cheap way of moving around.

Smooth grooves
Ancient Romans discovered that heavy carts wore grooves in their streets. They always drove in the grooves, as their carts ran more smoothly.

Getting around

About 200 years ago, most people travelled in wagons or stagecoaches pulled by horses. They were uncomfortable and could not carry much.

Barges on canals carried most goods. They carried more than wagons, but could not move quickly. Some took weeks to get from city to city.

Many people rode a horse or just walked. This was slow and risky. Robbers or highwaymen could attack them on the long, lonely roads between towns.

Running on rails

Carrying heavy loads was very difficult. About 250 years ago, miners in Europe laid two iron rails downhill from the mine to the nearest port. They discovered that wagons full of iron or coal ran much more easily on them. They emptied their load onto ships at the port. Horses could pull the empty cart back up to the mine again.

These early railways were often called wagonways.

Some wagons had a brake. The driver pulled it to stop.

Some wagons had ridges called flanges on their wheels. These fitted over the rail to keep the wheels running on them.

flange

A moving steam engine

An English blacksmith built the first engine powered by steam in 1712. His invention spread all over Europe.

Almost 100 years later, a man called Richard Trevithick built a steam engine that could move and pull loads.

In 1804, his engine pulled five loaded wagons and 70 people along two metal rails. This is how it worked.

The first passengers

In 1808, Trevithick built this round track in London. People paid to ride in a coach pulled by his steam engine called *Catch me who can*. They were the first passengers to pay to be pulled along by steam power.

This is the boiler. It has a metal tube covered with water inside it.

Steam comes out of the cylinder and goes up this chimney.

A fire burns in one end of the tube. Its fumes heat the tube up. The water around the hot tube turns it into steam.

The steam rushes into one end of this metal tube, called a cylinder.

The steam pushes against this sliding plug, called a piston.

cog

The piston is joined to these metal rods. As it slides up and down, they make a cog turn at the back of the engine.

The cog makes this big wheel turn.

main wheel

Two small toothed wheels turn with the big one. They move the main wheels forwards on the rails.

5

The first railways

By 1820, engineers all over Europe had begun to build moving steam engines. People called them locomotives. They tried out lots of different ideas to make them work better and go faster.

All about wheels

toothed wheel

This locomotive had a toothed wheel. The teeth fitted into grooves in an extra piece of track on the ground. As the wheel turned it helped pull the engine slowly forwards.

gear wheel

This steam locomotive ran on ordinary rails. Its wheels moved around when steam made smaller gear wheels turn. It ran well for over 50 years.

coupling rod   connecting rod

This engine was called the *Locomotion*. Rods called connecting rods linked one pair of wheels to the cylinders. All its wheels moved together as they were joined, or 'coupled', with coupling rods. An engineer called George Stephenson built it.

The Rainhill Trials
The Locomotive Competition

In 1829, a grand competition was held in Rainhill, England. Locomotives had to pass some tests to show which one worked best. They were called the Rainhill Trials.

Five locomotives entered the competition, but only three worked well enough to take part. They were called the *Rocket*, the *Sans Pareil* and the *Novelty*.

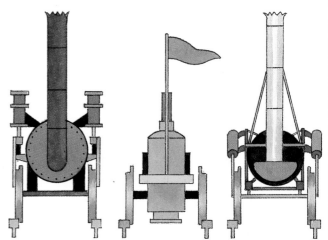

The *Sans Pareil* was entered by its builder, Timothy Hackworth.	Two engineers called Braithwaite and Ericsson built the *Novelty*.	The *Rocket* was built by George Stephenson and his son Robert.

To win the trials, the locomotives had to pull a 20 tonne (19.6 ton) load up and down a piece of track ten times. The total distance was 25km (15 miles).

The winner's reward

The winner of the Rainhill Trials would work on a new railway between the cities of Liverpool and Manchester. Factories would build other locomotives like it, too.

Manchester

Liverpool

Canal

railway

Sans Pareil

The *Sans Pareil* (which means 'without equal' in French), broke down after eight trips. Its boiler leaked.

Novelty

Most people wanted the *Novelty* to win, but it kept breaking down.

The *Rocket's* boiler had several tubes. They heated water more quickly than one tube.

Rocket

The Stephensons' *Rocket* was the winner. All steam locomotives built later had some of its features.

The steam rushed up these tubes into the chimney.

cylinder

This is the tender. It held coal for the fire and water for the boiler.

These are called carrying wheels. They help carry the weight of the locomotive.

connecting rod

This pair of big wheels are called the driving wheels. Connecting rods linked them straight to the cylinders.

Building a railway

Businessmen soon realised that they could make a lot of money if they built and ran a railway. They began building railways between towns and cities all over Europe.

Who built a railway?

First, a group of businessmen who wanted a railway formed a railway company. They raised the money for building work.

◀ They found an engineer to work out the best route for the railway. He planned exactly how to build it and how long it should take.

The engineer's plan ▶ was sent to the government to be studied. If the government gave its permission, work could start.

◀ Then the company paid a contractor to find men to do the building work. It took thousands of men to build each railway.

Once the men and ▶ the building materials arrived at the site, work began. It could go on for several years.

◀ When the railway was finished, the company officials held a huge banquet. The workers often had free beer and food.

Cuttings and embankments

Trains cannot travel up steep hills. The railway builders had to make the track as level as possible. They did this by making embankments and cuttings.

The builders dug a trough through hills. This was called a cutting. They laid the track on the bottom.

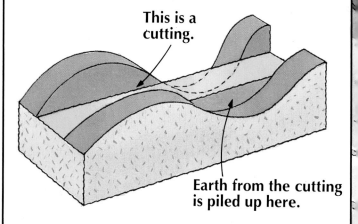

This is a cutting.

Earth from the cutting is piled up here.

They piled the earth and rock that they dug out to fill dips or valleys. This was called making an embankment.

At the cutting

The men who built the railways were often called navvies. They learnt their skills from the 'navigators' who built canals. Here, you can see them building a railway cutting.

pick

shovel

toolbox

brace and bit

The navvies emptied their barrows at the top.

A horse walked around this machine, called a horse gin. This wound up a rope fixed to the navvy's barrow.

It pulled the navvy and his barrow up the side of the cutting.

The navvies lived in tents by the building site.

Some cuttings were over 18m (59ft) deep.

Gangers

Some early railway builders were called gangers. They travelled around with their tools, looking for work. This was called tramping.

barrow

rope

ramp

Laying the track

The navvies spread broken stones called ballast over the ground. This made a flat base for the railway to go on.

They laid wooden planks called sleepers on top. Then, the navvies screwed clips called chairs onto both ends.

chair

rail

key

The rails slotted into the clips or chairs. Wooden wedges called keys kept them in place.

9

Railway madness

The first railways were very successful. In the 1840s, companies built many more. Some newspapers called it the age of 'Railway Mania', or railway madness. For many people, life was never the same again once the railways began to spread.

Riches from railways

The engineers, George and Robert Stephenson, became rich. Their factory built locomotives to run on new railways all over the world. This one is called *der Adler* (*the Eagle*). It worked on the first German railway in 1835.

Some railway contractors made huge fortunes. The most successful was Thomas Brassey. He was in charge of over 75,000 navvies around the world at one time.

Ordinary people bought shares in railways. This means they gave the companies money to help build a railway in exchange for a share of the money it made when it was finished. ▶

Against the railways

Not everybody did well from the spread of the railways.

Many coach drivers and canal bargemen lost their jobs. The railway had taken their trade.

Some railways went over farming land. Landowners and farmers were angry. Many houses were destroyed during railway building work, too.

The gauges problem

The distance between the two rails of a railway track is called the gauge. The first railways were built before engineers had agreed on the best one, so some had a different gauge from others. Trains could not run on both of them. In Britain, this caused a big argument.

The most common gauge was 4ft 8½ in (1.43m). This was called standard gauge. A British engineer called Brunel laid track 7ft ¼ in (2.14m) apart. This was called broad gauge.

When the two gauges met, all the passengers and goods had to change trains. British engineers argued for over 50 years before choosing standard gauge in 1892. Some countries still have mixed gauges today.

These driving wheels are over 2.4m (8ft) high.

This is a broad gauge locomotive. It was built specially to run on broad gauge tracks.

Travelling by train

By the 1850s, people could travel in three classes of railway carriage. They were not mixed in one train at first. Rich people paid much more to travel in comfort.

First class carriages were the most expensive. They looked like rich peoples' coaches.

Second class carriages had wooden seats. Most had a roof to protect the passengers.

Third class tickets were the cheapest. The carriages often had no roofs or seats.

At this time, the railways made most of their money by transporting goods. They began to build different sorts of railway wagons to carry different goods.

British engineers spread the gauges problems to lands in the British Empire, such as India and Australia.

In some countries, the gauges problem was solved by laying two sets of tracks. Both sorts of locomotive could run on them.

The place where the gauges met was called the 'break of gauge'.

This is a standard gauge locomotive.

Railroads in North America

In America, railways were called railroads. Once they were built, people could travel the long distances between cities much more comfortably and quickly than before. The railroads were planned and built very quickly. They had a lot of curves and hills and the track was laid with no ballast underneath it. American locomotives had to be specially adapted to run on them.

The American *Standard*

Engineers began building locomotives like this near New York, in 1855. They designed them to be able to cope with the difficult conditions of the American railroads. People called this type of locomotive the American *Standard*.

American locomotives were often richly decorated.

Logs for the fire and water for the boiler were kept in the tender.

The driving wheels are coupled so they move together. This helped them grip the rails better and climb slopes.

Swivelling bogies

Early locomotives slipped off the rails going round curves on the railroads. Engineers had to solve this problem.

A trolley with four small wheels was fixed underneath the front of locomotives. It was called a truck or bogie.

Bogies could swivel from side to side and gently lead the locomotive around curves. They soon spread to many countries.

bogie

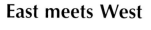

East meets West

The railroad from the East to West coast is 2,820km (1,750 miles) long.

Two teams of thousands of navvies took seven years to build a railroad across America from East to West.

They started from opposite coasts. On 10 May 1869, the two teams finally met at Promontory Point, Utah.

This is a smokestack. It had a wire net inside it to catch burning wood sparks.

Burning sparks

Most locomotives in America burned wood not coal. On this early engine, sparks from the chimney set fire to passengers' clothes.

Large headlights helped the driver see ahead on remote parts of the railroad.

The boiler of American locomotives was a bit thinner at the front. This put most of its weight on the large driving wheels and less on the small bogie wheels.

This is a cowcatcher. Railroads had no fences around them. The cowcatcher pushed stray animals off the track.

These are the bogie wheels.

Bringing changes

The railroads were very important. Life in the West of America changed quickly after they were built.

Thousands of people from all over the world went to farm the rich land on the prairies.

Settlers and railway builders stole many of the Red Indians' hunting grounds.

Passengers on the railroads shot thousands of wild buffalo. Today, they are rare.

Bigger and better

By 1860, thousands of people worked for railway companies, doing many different jobs. Engineers were designing bigger, better steam locomotives too.

Railway jobs

Railway workers had to learn skills that had not even existed 50 years earlier. Here are some of the jobs people did on the railways.

◄ The driver rode on the footplate at the back of the engine. He drove the locomotive.

◄ The fireman shovelled coal into the firebox. He also checked that the boiler had enough water in it.

The station master was in charge of running the station. ▶

The guard made ▶ sure the passengers and goods were safely on the train.

The porter helped ▶ load and unload luggage for passengers.

◄ The booking clerk sold tickets. He also read the timetable and told passengers the times of trains.

◄ The signalman controlled the signals that told trains when to stop or go.

◄ Gangs of platelayers repaired the railway track.

Railway signals

When railway lines began to cross each other, there was more danger of accidents. Train drivers needed signals beside the track to show when the line was clear. Here are some of the most common ones.

◄ These signals were called semaphore signals. They could be set in different positions. Each one had a different meaning.

At first, special railway ▶ policemen held up flags as signals. Each flag position meant something different.

By 1850, all the signals for a ▶ stretch of track were controlled from a hut called a signalbox beside the track.

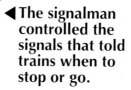
◄ Soon, railway companies paid signalmen to control wooden signals on top of a post. They used levers to move them up and down.

◄ By the 1860s, signalmen used electric telegraph machines to tell each other when a train was approaching their box.

On the footplate

Here is a locomotive built in about 1850. You can see that engineers had improved steam engines in many ways since the *Rocket* in 1829.

This weatherboard protects the engine driver from wind, smoke and rain.

This whistle warns people and other trains to clear the track.

This is the regulator handle. The driver used it to control how much steam went into the cylinders.

This gauge shows how much water was in the boiler.

This safety valve lets out steam if too much is collecting in the boiler.

This is the smokebox. Smoke passes through here before going up the chimney.

This is a blastpipe. It takes steam from the cylinders up the chimney.

The cylinders are built into the frame of the locomotive.

Changing the points

Where railway tracks crossed, trains could change onto another line. Signalmen pulled levers at places called points to set the track in the right position for a train.

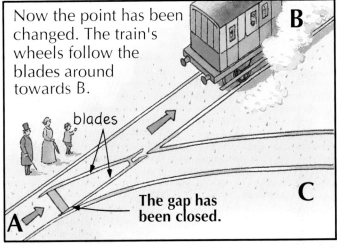

A train is coming from A. The blades of this point have been set so that they guide the wheels to C.

These are the blades.

The train's wheels cannot jump over this gap.

B

C

A

Now the point has been changed. The train's wheels follow the blades around towards B.

blades

The gap has been closed.

B

C

A

Tunnels and bridges

Sometimes, railways had to go under mountains or under water. The navvies had to dig tunnels. They also built bridges to carry trains over rivers and deep valleys.

Tunnelling under mountains

The Alps mountains stopped trains travelling easily across Europe. Tunnelling under them was the most difficult and dangerous job the navvies faced. Between 1871 and 1922, they built five tunnels under the Alps.

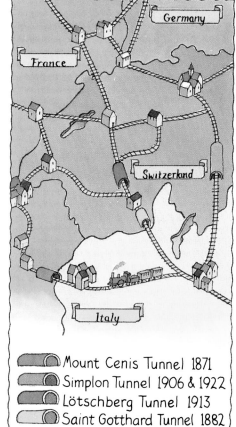

Meeting in the middle

The navvies started digging on both sides of the mountain the tunnel was to go through. They dug towards each other.

They used picks, dynamite and powerful drills to blast through rock. Many men died in accidents during the work.

After several years, the two sides of the tunnel joined. Navvies could then lay the track for trains.

Mount Cenis Tunnel 1871
Simplon Tunnel 1906 & 1922
Lötschberg Tunnel 1913
Saint Gotthard Tunnel 1882

The Severn Tunnel

Building tunnels under water was very dangerous. The tunnel under the River Severn between England and Wales flooded five times before it was finished in 1886.

The Severn Tunnel is almost 8km (5 miles) long. It took 3,500 men over 12 years to build it. They lined the inside of the tunnel with bricks to keep water out.

The navvies used over 75,000 bricks to line the inside of the tunnel.

Two sets of tracks go through the tunnel. Trains travel in both directions.

16

Railway bridges

Railway bridges are built of different things, in many styles, around the world. The bridges made of steel are probably the most famous.

The Forth Bridge

The Forth Bridge stretches over 2km (1.2 miles) of water in Scotland called the Firth of Forth. The bridge is made of steel tubes. It took seven years to build. The first locomotive ran across it in 1890.

Trestle bridges

Where timber was plentiful, people built wooden railway bridges. They were called trestle bridges. In India, ants ate the timber and some bridges collapsed.

The bridge-builders used over 54,000 tonnes (53,000 tons) of steel.

4,600 men built the bridge. They were called briggers. 57 briggers died during the building work.

This part of the bridge was built on an island in the middle of the Firth.

— crane

There are two sets of railway tracks across the bridge.

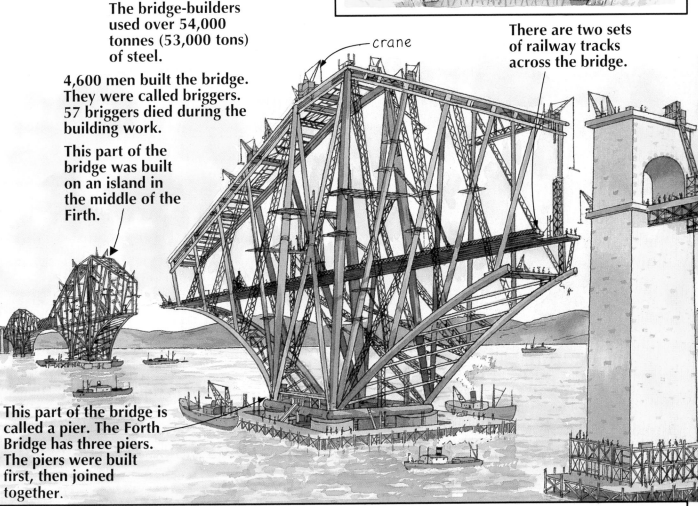

This part of the bridge is called a pier. The Forth Bridge has three piers. The piers were built first, then joined together.

Viaducts

Some valleys were too deep to fill with earth to keep the railway level. Bridges called viaducts were built over them. They had lots of brick or stone arches.

Some European viaducts had over 30 arches.

The word viaduct comes from the Latin for 'a way over'.

17

Railways around the world

The first railways were built in Europe and North America. Once they were running smoothly, their engineers went to countries such as Africa, Asia, Russia and South America to build railways there. They faced a new set of problems.

The riches of South America

There were silver and copper mines high in the Andes Mountains in Peru. In 1870, navvies began building a railway between the mines and the ports on the coast.

The line took over 23 years to finish. Engineers laid the track in zigzags so that the locomotives could climb the steep mountain slopes. This is how they did it.

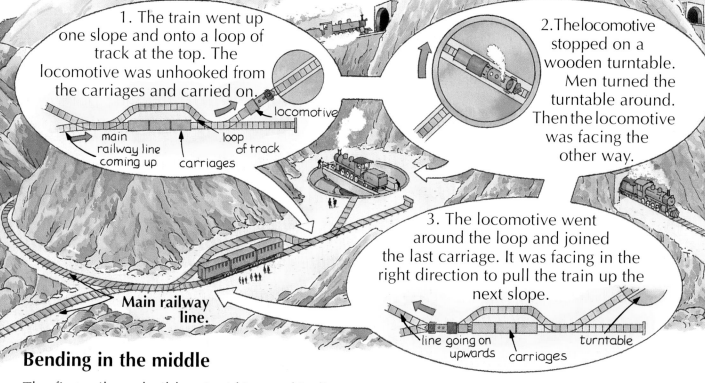

1. The train went up one slope and onto a loop of track at the top. The locomotive was unhooked from the carriages and carried on.

main railway line coming up   carriages   loop of track   locomotive

2. The locomotive stopped on a wooden turntable. Men turned the turntable around. Then the locomotive was facing the other way.

3. The locomotive went around the loop and joined the last carriage. It was facing in the right direction to pull the train up the next slope.

line going on upwards   carriages   turntable

Main railway line.

Bending in the middle

The first railway-builders in Africa and India had to lay track over deserts, swamps and huge plains. They did not lay much ballast and used light, steel rails. Engineers built a new sort of locomotive that would be heavy enough to grip these light rails while pulling huge loads. They were called articulated locomotives.

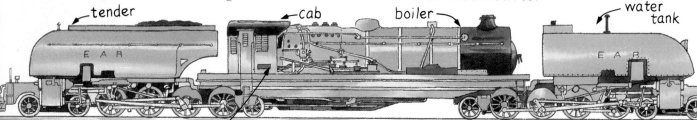

tender   cab   boiler   water tank

This articulated locomotive was designed by H.W. Garratt in 1929.

Articulated locomotives had three parts. The water tank and tender for fuel were built on top of engine frames. The huge boiler was in the middle, with the cab.

As the three parts of these huge locomotives were separate, they bent like elbows as they went round corners. This stopped the train coming off the rails.

Garratt's articulated locomotives bend like this when they go around corners.

Trans-Siberian Railway

In 1891, the Tsar of Russia ordered a railway to be built between the cities of Moscow and Vladivostock. It had to cross mountains, icy plains, lakes, rivers and bogs. It would be called the Trans-Siberian Railway.

The first train went from Moscow to Vladivostock in 1901. A ferry carried it across Lake Baikal.

That winter, the lake froze. Rails were laid on top of the ice for trains to run on. The ice cracked and a train sank.

In 1904, builders laid railway tracks along the steep cliffs around the lake. The whole journey now takes seven days.

Driving power

Only reliable, powerful engines ran on the icy Trans-Siberian Railway. Some of the most famous were the *P36* type locomotives, like this one. They only stopped work in 1976.

If the *P36* ran out of fuel, it was left at a station. A new engine was fixed to the front of the train. Once, it took 19 engines to cover the whole Trans-Siberian route.

These panels are called smoke deflectors. They push smoke away from the driver's cab so that he can see ahead.

This powerful light helps the driver see in dark, dangerous weather.

Rails on Russian railways are further apart than in most countries. Taller, heavier trains can run on them.

Building a steam locomotive

By the end of the 1800s, factories were building locomotives all over Europe. They were called locomotive works. Thousands of people got jobs in the works and brand new towns were built for them to live in.

They built locomotives in many sizes and styles. It took hundreds of skilled workers to make each one. Different parts of the engine were built in different rooms inside the huge locomotive works.

Inside the locomotive work

◀ 1. Workers made the cylinders, wheels and many other parts of the locomotive in a room called the foundry. They poured hot metal into moulds shaped like the engine part. When the metal cooled, they tipped it out and smoothed off rough edges. The parts had to be exactly the right shape.

2. They made the metal frame of the locomotive in a room called the machine shop. Workers cut the frame out of sheets of solid steel. Then they drilled holes so that the frame could be fitted together with bolts. Other parts were cut out here, too. ▶

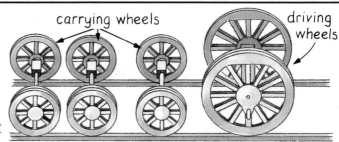

3. The boiler was made in the boiler shop. The workers rolled sheets of steel into the right curved shape while the metal was hot. Then they fixed the cooled sheets together with bolts called rivets. Next they made the firebox and riveted that into place.

Wheel arrangements

By 1900, many different sizes of locomotive ran on railways around the world. They often had different numbers of driving wheels and smaller carrying wheels, arranged in a different order. This is called their wheel arrangement.

In 1900, a man called Frederick Whyte invented this system of numbers to describe the wheel arrangements of steam locomotives. It is still used today.

carrying wheels

driving wheels

This locomotive has a 6-2-0 wheel arrangement. It has six carrying wheels (6) in front of two driving wheels (2). There are no more carrying wheels behind them (0).

4. They took all the parts to the erecting shop. The builders fitted the cylinders into the frame first. Then a crane lowered the boiler down and the men bolted it in place. ▼

5. The crane ▶ lifted the locomotive again. Two men slid each pair of wheels into place. Then they fitted the coupling and connecting rods to all the wheels. Lastly, they checked that all the steam pipes were fitted properly.

6. The cab was put together ▶ on its own. The builders fixed it in place and checked the controls. They painted the locomotive the colours the customer wanted. This was called the livery. Once they had tested the new engine, it left the factory to start work on the railway.

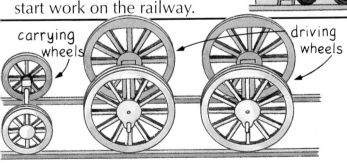

carrying wheels driving wheels carrying wheels driving wheels carrying wheels

This is a 2-4-0 locomotive. It has two carrying wheels (2) in front of four driving wheels (4). There are no wheels behind them (0).

This 4-2-2 has two huge driving wheels (2) behind four carrying wheels (4). There are two more carrying wheels under the cab (2).

Luxury on rails

Gradually, railway companies began to build more comfortable carriages for their passengers. They realized that people would pay more to travel in them. By 1900, it was fashionable for the rich and famous to travel on luxurious trains.

The Pullman carriage

In 1859, an American furniture-maker called George Pullman built a new sort of railway carriage. His idea was so successful that it soon spread to Europe, too.

During the day, Pullman's carriage had soft seats and a corridor up the middle. Passengers could walk about.

At night, bunk beds folded down from above the seats. Seats became beds, too. Curtains kept them private.

Day

Night

The *Orient Express*

A Belgian called Georges Nagelmackers set up a company called the Compagnie Internationale des Wagons-Lits (International Company of Sleeping Cars). It ran luxurious trains across Europe.

In 1883, Nagelmackers advertised a four day journey from Paris to Istanbul. Most of the journey was on a train called the *Orient Express*. Its first dining carriage looked something like this inside.

The route of the Orient Express

Paris — Munich — Vienna — Budapest — Belgrade — Constantinople

This is a library and smoking room for men on board the *Orient Express*.

The inside of the restaurant carriage was richly decorated with carvings, soft fabric and gold.

Waiters in uniforms served the passengers all their meals.

People said the carriage went around corners so smoothly that waiters did not spill a drop of soup.

Comfortable carriages

Railway companies began to be proud of the comfort they offered their passengers. Based on Pullman's ideas, they built several sorts of comfortable carriages.

Some carriages were split into rooms called compartments. Some passengers preferred compartments to carriages with corridors.

This is a saloon car. Passengers could relax on soft sofas in them and men could smoke. A family often booked a whole saloon car to itself.

At first, passengers on long journeys had to gobble a meal at a station while the train waited. Gradually, more trains had dining carriages.

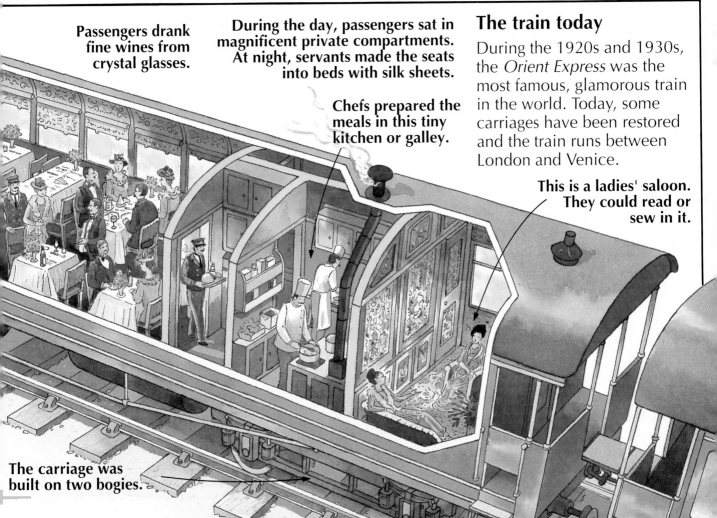

Passengers drank fine wines from crystal glasses.

During the day, passengers sat in magnificent private compartments. At night, servants made the seats into beds with silk sheets.

Chefs prepared the meals in this tiny kitchen or galley.

The train today

During the 1920s and 1930s, the *Orient Express* was the most famous, glamorous train in the world. Today, some carriages have been restored and the train runs between London and Venice.

This is a ladies' saloon. They could read or sew in it.

The carriage was built on two bogies.

Steaming for speed

Towards the end of the 1800s, inventors were trying out new sorts of engines. Steam locomotive builders were worried. They began building locomotives to go faster than ever before. Today, some of the locomotives they built are very famous.

Flying Scotsman

This locomotive is called *Flying Scotsman*. It was built in Britain in 1923 to pull the express train from London to Scotland. It is preserved and still runs today.

These are called superheater tubes. They heat steam in the boiler a second time. This makes it hotter and even more powerful.

This wide blastpipe takes steam from the cylinders up the chimney.

Going faster

Flying Scotsman could pick up more water and change its crew without stopping. This saved time on journeys.

A scoop came down ▶ from under the locomotive's tender. It scooped up water from a trough between the tracks as the train raced along.

scoop

corridor

◀ A second crew rode in a carriage on board. When the first crew got tired, the new crew came through a corridor in the side of the tender to start work.

Mallard

In the 1930s, a British engineer ▶ called Gresley built this locomotive, called *Mallard*. It holds the world record for the fastest steam locomotive ever. It reached 202.7kph (126mph).

Mallard is streamlined. This means it is specially shaped to cut through wind and go faster.

Mallard was one of a famous series of locomotives called A4s

Mallard pulled trains full of tourists until 1988.

These driving wheels are almost 2m (6ft 8in) high. That is taller than most men.

Inside the cab

This is what the *Flying Scotsman's* cab looks like inside.

This is the steam pressure gauge.

Driving an express train was a skilful job. The fireman had to keep exactly the right steam pressure in the boiler all the time, too.

These are seats for the driver and fireman.

This arch of bricks helps spread the fire's heat all around the firebox.

Small holes called valves let steam in and out of the cylinders at exactly the right time.

These rods move together to make sure the locomotive's wheels go around quickly and smoothly.

Smoke from the chimney rushed over *Mallard's* streamlined body.

MALLARD

Shaped for speed

The chimneys and cabs of many locomotives stuck out. The wind could not flow over them quickly. So the train lost some speed.

Gresley tested streamlined engines. He found that the wind rushed over them and the train did not lose speed. Most trains today are streamlined.

These streamlined wheel covers are called valances.

The diesel train

Today, steam trains no longer run on main railways. New sorts of train have replaced them. One of these is the diesel train. Diesel trains get power from an engine invented by Dr Rudolf Diesel in Germany 1892. At that time, they were less expensive to run than steam engines. By 1960, there were only a few steam trains left.

How a diesel engine works

Most diesel locomotives are called diesel electrics. They have three main parts. These are a diesel engine, an electric generator and one or more motors. All three parts work together to make the locomotive move. Here is what they do.

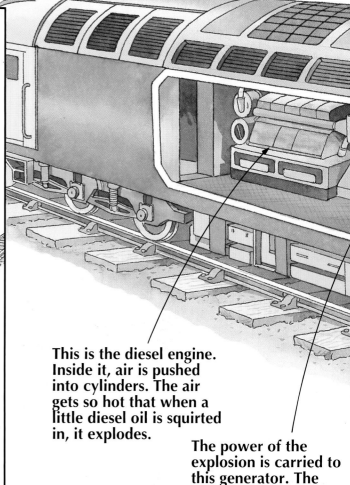

This is the diesel engine. Inside it, air is pushed into cylinders. The air gets so hot that when a little diesel oil is squirted in, it explodes.

The power of the explosion is carried to this generator. The generator turns it into electricity.

Diesel speed

During the 1920s and 1930s, railways tried out diesel engines to see how fast they could go. They found they set new speed records.

Flying Hamburger

This diesel train is called *Flying Hamburger*. It had a diesel engine, generator and motor fixed under each of its two carriages for extra power.

In 1939, it reached 214kph (133.5mph) between Berlin and Hamburg in Germany. This set a new world record for rail speed.

Zephyrs

American engineers streamlined some diesel locomotives with stainless steel panels. They were called *Zephyrs* and could reach speeds of 177kph (109mph).

More than one

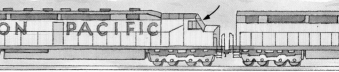

There is no driver in this cab.

Diesel engines are often joined together to give more pulling power. This is called working in multiple. Two diesel engines are

Inside the cab

This is what a diesel engine's cab looks like inside. It is much more comfortable than a steam locomotive cab. The driver works on his own as there is no need for a fireman.

Brake handles

Speedometer

Buttons to start and stop the engine.

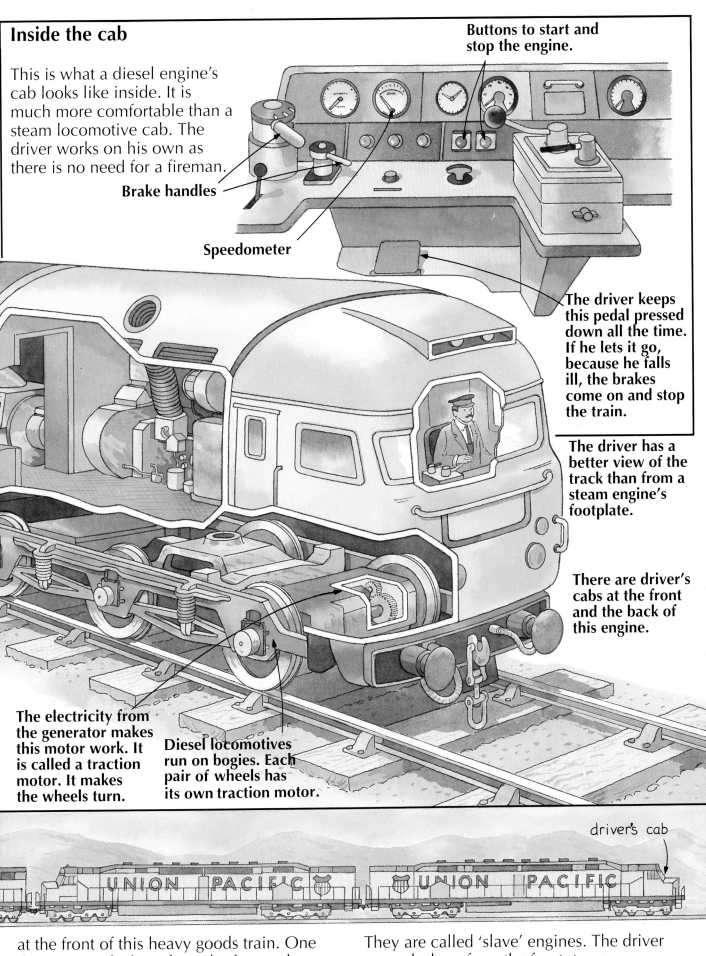

The driver keeps this pedal pressed down all the time. If he lets it go, because he falls ill, the brakes come on and stop the train.

The driver has a better view of the track than from a steam engine's footplate.

There are driver's cabs at the front and the back of this engine.

The electricity from the generator makes this motor work. It is called a traction motor. It makes the wheels turn.

Diesel locomotives run on bogies. Each pair of wheels has its own traction motor.

driver's cab

UNION PACIFIC

UNION PACIFIC

at the front of this heavy goods train. One driver controls them from the front cab. Engines are also put between goods wagons.

They are called 'slave' engines. The driver controls them from the front, too.

Electric trains

The fastest trains in the world run on electricity. Electric trains cannot run on ordinary railway tracks. They get power from a third rail carrying electricity or from a cable hung above the track.

Building electric railways is expensive but most countries think it is worth it. They are adapting their railways so that electric trains can run on them because they are fast, quiet and smoke-free.

Tiny train

A German inventor called Siemens built the first electric train in 1879. It pulled about 30 people along a track at a big exhibition in Berlin. Bunches of copper wire under the train brushed against an electric rail. They took electric power to a motor above the wheels. This motor made the wheels turn and the locomotive moved forwards.

Inside an electric train

Bombing damaged most of Europe's railways during the Second World War. They had to be rebuilt afterwards. In many countries, the new railways were built for electric trains like this to run on them.

This is the pantograph. It rubs against the cable and picks up electricity as the train moves.

Electric cables hang from masts, or pylons, above the track.

driver's cab

Oil in here cools the transfomer down if it gets too hot.

These motors make the wheels turn. They are called traction motors.

Electricity is carried to this box, called the transformer. It sends electricity to motors above the wheels.

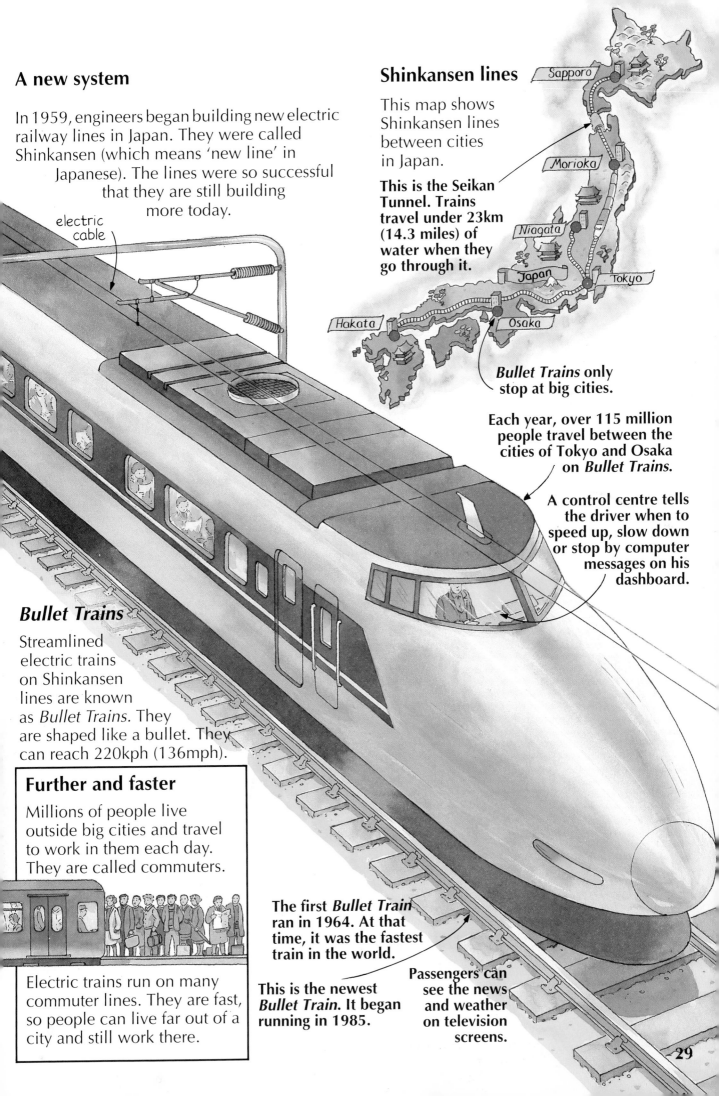

A new system

In 1959, engineers began building new electric railway lines in Japan. They were called Shinkansen (which means 'new line' in Japanese). The lines were so successful that they are still building more today.

electric cable

Shinkansen lines

This map shows Shinkansen lines between cities in Japan.

This is the Seikan Tunnel. Trains travel under 23km (14.3 miles) of water when they go through it.

Sapporo

Morioka

Niagata

Japan

Tokyo

Hakata

Osaka

Bullet Trains only stop at big cities.

Each year, over 115 million people travel between the cities of Tokyo and Osaka on *Bullet Trains*.

A control centre tells the driver when to speed up, slow down or stop by computer messages on his dashboard.

Bullet Trains

Streamlined electric trains on Shinkansen lines are known as *Bullet Trains*. They are shaped like a bullet. They can reach 220kph (136mph).

Further and faster

Millions of people live outside big cities and travel to work in them each day. They are called commuters.

Electric trains run on many commuter lines. They are fast, so people can live far out of a city and still work there.

The first *Bullet Train* ran in 1964. At that time, it was the fastest train in the world.

This is the newest *Bullet Train*. It began running in 1985.

Passengers can see the news and weather on television screens.

29

Special trains

Ordinary trains have always carried passengers and freight from place to place.

Some trains are special because they have more unusual jobs to do.

Royal trains

By 1840, even kings and queens felt it was safe to ride on the railway. Many countries built luxurious trains for them to travel in. This one was built for Queen Victoria of England in 1869.

Curtains hid the Queen from view if she did not want to wave at people.

Thick carpets and cushions helped keep the carriage warm.

Royal trains were the only trains that had toilets until the middle of the 1800s. Even they were richly decorated.

Mail by rail

Trains called mail trains carry letters and parcels quickly and cheaply. Moving mail from place to place has always been an important job for the railways.

Until the 1970s, bags of mail dropped into a rope bag on the side of one carriage as the train passed. Today, mail is put on the train at a station.

On board the fast night mail train, people work through the night, sorting out mail. These carriages are called Travelling Post Offices (TPOs).

In some cities, mail travels between main railway stations on underground trains. The trains have no driver. Electric signals control them.

Trains at war

Trains were very important during the two World Wars. Many railways were bombed by enemies. This kept from trains moving weapons, troops and supplies around.

◄ Some railway carriages became moving hospitals to bring wounded men home. The seats were made into beds. Doctors and nurses rode on board.

Trains carried millions of children called evacuees to spend the war in the country. People hoped the evacuees would be safer there, as planes mostly bombed cities. ►

Trips by train

In 1841, an Englishman called Thomas Cook offered cheap tickets for a day trip, or excursion, on a train. He sold them all easily.

Excursions soon became popular all over Europe. They gave people in cities the chance to see the sea or some countryside.

Excursion trains were often called 'specials'.

Rail excursions also took people to horse races, exhibitions, or political meetings.

Few people had cars until the 1940s. Colourful posters like this told people how easy it was to take a trip by train.

~ The ~
Grand Railway
Excursion

If a passenger on an excursion missed the train back, he had to pay a full fare on another train.

Trains in cities

Big cities have always been railway centres. All important lines begin and end in them.

There are even railways under the streets of many big cities.

Going underground

By 1860, London's streets were clogged up with people and traffic. Engineers planned underground railways to carry passengers.

They built them in two different ways. The first was called cut and cover. In the second, workers used a metal shield to protect them.

Cut and cover

The builders dug a cutting through each street. They laid railway tracks on the bottom and built a roof to make a tunnel.

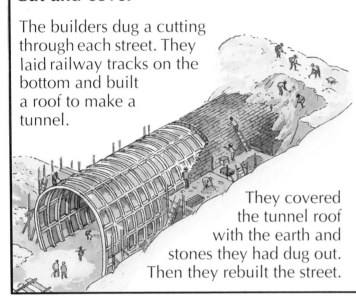

They covered the tunnel roof with the earth and stones they had dug out. Then they rebuilt the street.

The Greathead shield

Cut and cover blocked streets during building work. In 1870, an engineer called Henry Greathead invented a way of tunnelling under the ground.

Metal ribs and panels

The men stood inside a metal tube, or shield. The shield held the tunnel roof up as they dug. It moved slowly forwards.

Early trains   This electric train ran on the underground in London in 1890. Its carriage had no windows. Engineers thought passengers might be scared if they saw tunnel walls.

No 31

A guard stood on this platform and shouted out the names of stations.

Electricity travels along this metal rail.

This is called a shoe. As the train moves, it touches the electric rail and collects electricity.

The electricity is carried to motors under here. They make the wheels turn.

Underground trains today

Today, underground trains around the world carry millions of passengers every day. They work in the same way they did 100 years ago, but they are more comfortable.

Trains like this run on the underground system, or *Métro*, in Paris today.

The carriage doors open and close automatically.

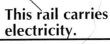

This shows where the train is going.

974 TERMINUS MARIE DE MONTREUL

Some *Métro* trains have rubber tyres like these. They help them run smoothly and slow down quickly.

The tyres are changed after the train has done about 450,000km (279,624 miles).

This rail carries electricity.

Railway stations

In many cities, grand stations show how proud the builders were of their railway systems.

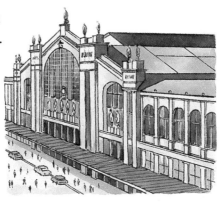

In the 1900s, many stations had huge arched roofs made of iron ribs. There were panes of glass between each rib.

Architects often tried out their new ideas on railway stations. Some looked like palaces or cathedrals.

In Moscow, many of the underground stations are richly decorated and lit by chandeliers.

Freight on rails

The first railways proved to tradesmen that trains could move goods quickly and cheaply. Today, railways make most of their money from goods, or freight.

Trains carry goods in specially-built wagons, or metal boxes called containers. Freight trains can carry more than trucks. They help to keep roads clear of traffic.

Marshalling yards

This is a marshalling yard. Freight trains are made up of wagons which are going to the same destination. The wagons are sorted into trains on pieces of track called sidings at huge yards like this one in North America.

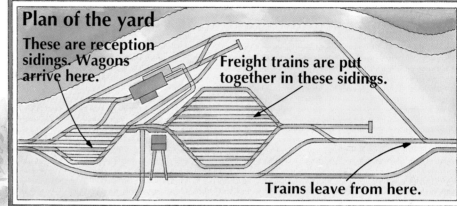

Plan of the yard

These are reception sidings. Wagons arrive here.

Freight trains are put together in these sidings.

Trains leave from here.

shunter

This is the control tower.

This is the engine repair shed.

1. Loaded wagons arrive at one side of the yard. A locomotive called a shunter pushes them gently over a small hill called a hump.

shunter

hump

2. The wagon rolls downhill. A small camera reads a label on its side. This tells a computer in the control tower what freight the wagon is carrying.

3. The controller sets the points on the tracks so the wagon rolls onto the right siding. Brakes in the track, called retarders slow it down.

retarders

Moving freight

Today, ships, trucks and trains work together to move freight to where it is needed.

At docks, huge cranes can lift containers of freight from ships straight onto a train or from a train onto a ship. They do not need unpacking.

Companies can hire a whole train of wagons to move a large amount of freight. These trains are called 'block' trains.

The backs of trucks can be loaded onto flat freight wagons. This saves fuel and a long drive by road. This is called the 'piggyback' system.

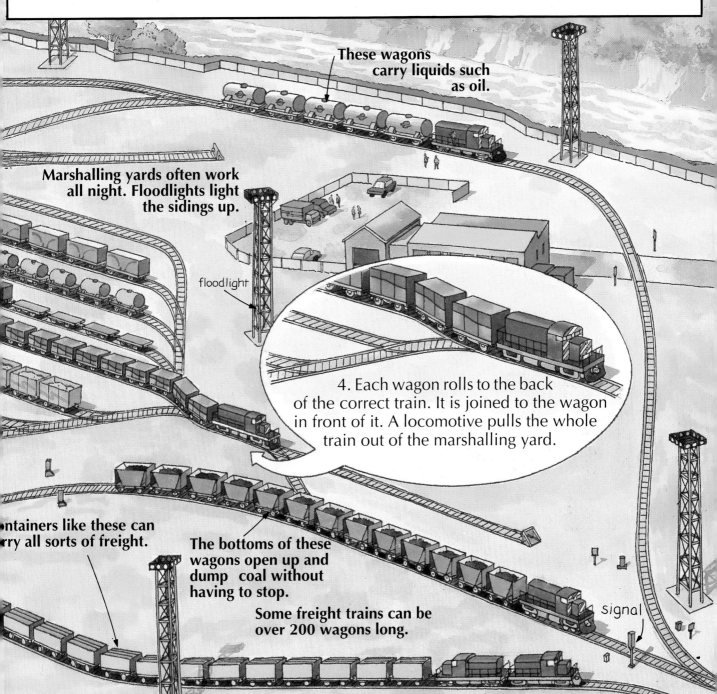

These wagons carry liquids such as oil.

Marshalling yards often work all night. Floodlights light the sidings up.

floodlight

4. Each wagon rolls to the back of the correct train. It is joined to the wagon in front of it. A locomotive pulls the whole train out of the marshalling yard.

ntainers like these can rry all sorts of freight.

The bottoms of these wagons open up and dump coal without having to stop.

Some freight trains can be over 200 wagons long.

signal

Unusual trains and railways

Some trains do not look like ordinary trains at all. They are built to work on unusual railways or to do special sorts of work.

One of their main jobs is to keep the railway track in good condition for trains to run safely on it.

Ballast cleaning train

The small stones, or ballast, underneath railway sleepers should make a level base. Trains passing over it can make it uneven and dirty.

This train scoops up ballast, cleans it and puts it back under the tracks in a smooth layer. It is called a ballast cleaning train.

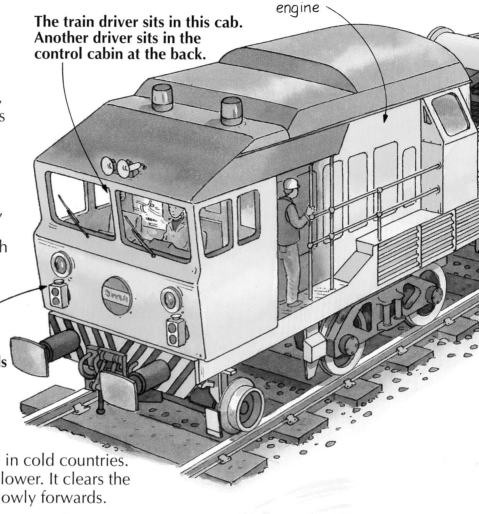

The train driver sits in this cab. Another driver sits in the control cabin at the back.

diesel engine

The ballast cleaning train moves forwards very slowly.

Snow blower

Snow often blocks railways in cold countries. This train is called a snowblower. It clears the track of snow as it moves slowly forwards.

This huge propeller spins around. It sucks snow in.

diesel engine

Powerful fans blow the snow out of this tube, away from the track.

This blade cuts through snow on the tracks, too.

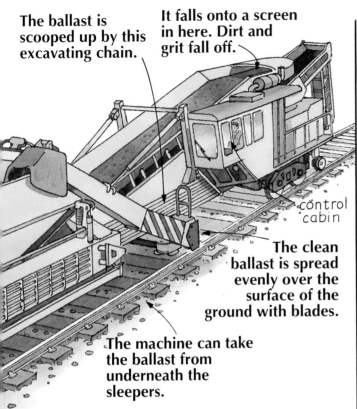

The ballast is scooped up by this excavating chain.

It falls onto a screen in here. Dirt and grit fall off.

control cabin

The clean ballast is spread evenly over the surface of the ground with blades.

The machine can take the ballast from underneath the sleepers.

Rail crane

An obstacle on the track is very dangerous. Other trains could be delayed by it or crash into it. Signalmen call for rail cranes like this to clear the line.

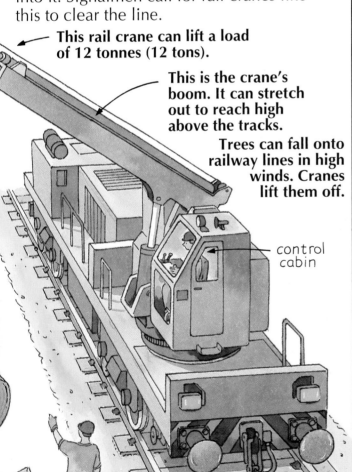

This rail crane can lift a load of 12 tonnes (12 tons).

This is the crane's boom. It can stretch out to reach high above the tracks.

Trees can fall onto railway lines in high winds. Cranes lift them off.

control cabin

Mountain railways

Some railways are built to climb mountains or steep slopes. Ordinary trains cannot do this. Their wheels would slip.

Rack and pinion railway

In 1870, a Swiss engineer called Riggenbach built a railway up a mountainside. It was called a rack and pinion railway. Many railways like it are still running today.

Pinion wheels have teeth all the way around the edge.

This steam locomotive makes the pinion wheel turn.

pinion wheel

This is the rack. As the pinion wheel turns, its teeth slot into these gaps. This pulls the train up the slope.

Funicular railways

Railways called funiculars can go up even steeper slopes than a rack and pinion train. Cables pull them up and down.

A loop of metal cable is fixed between the top and bottom of the slope. Two carriages, called cars, start at opposite ends of the loop.

cable

As the car at the top goes slowly downhill, its weight pulls the cable down. This hauls the second car up the other side of the slope.

Trains of today

Railways today try to run fast, efficient train services so that passengers will travel by train and not by plane or car.

Trains travel faster than ever before. Tracks, signals and the skills of train drivers have to keep improving, too.

pantograph

Speed and comfort

Passengers on important rail routes in Europe now travel in fast express trains. They expect comfortable carriages and trains that are on time. Here are two examples.

This streamlined diesel train runs on British railways. It is called the *HST*, which stands for *High Speed Train*. *HSTs* can reach speeds of 200kph (125mph).

Electric trains like this began running on railways in Germany in 1990. They are called the *Inter City Express (ICE)*. *ICE* trains can reach 249kph (155mph).

The *TGV*

This is the *TGV* (Train à Grande Vitesse, which means High Speed Train in French). *TGVs* first ran on French railways in 1981. In 1990, this new version of the train called the *TGV Atlantic* became the fastest passenger train in the world. It reached 515kph (320mph) in a test.

TGVs are only allowed to travel at a speed of 300kph (186mph) on French railways.

pantograph

There is an electric locomotive, or power unit, at the front and the back of each *TGV* train.

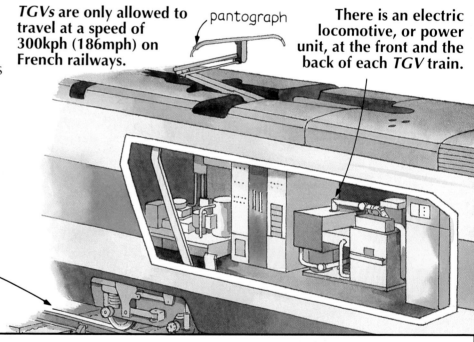

TGVs run best on specially built railway tracks but they can run on ordinary ones, too.

On board a *TGV*

Waiters serve meals to first class passengers as they sit in their comfortable seats.

Other passengers can buy and eat a snack as they watch videos in this carriage.

Passengers can telephone anywhere in the world from on board a *TGV*.

Modern signalling

Today, several signalmen often work in big signalboxes called power boxes. They control all the hundreds of signals and points along a large area of railway track. Inside each powerbox is a big diagram of all the track it controls. This in how signalmen use this diagram to set the signals and points for each train.

1. Lit-up numbers in these boxes tell the signalman a train is approaching and where it needs to go.

Signal →

2. He sets the signals by pressing buttons on the diagram. The train's route lights up with white lights.

3. As the train passes, the white lights turn red. This shows the signalman that that piece of track is busy.

4. Once the train has passed safely, the signalman presses a button to show him the line is clear for another train.

Over 500 passengers can travel on a *TGV*.

Computers send messages to the cab to tell the driver when to speed up, slow down and stop.

Many people now travel on the *TGV* instead of on planes.

SNCF

It would take the *TGV* 3.3km (2 miles) to stop if it braked when travelling at its normal speed.

Computers check the *TGV's* brakes as it speeds along.

The world by train

Today, you can travel all over the world by train. This map shows some of the many famous or unusual trains to watch for on a railway tour of the world.

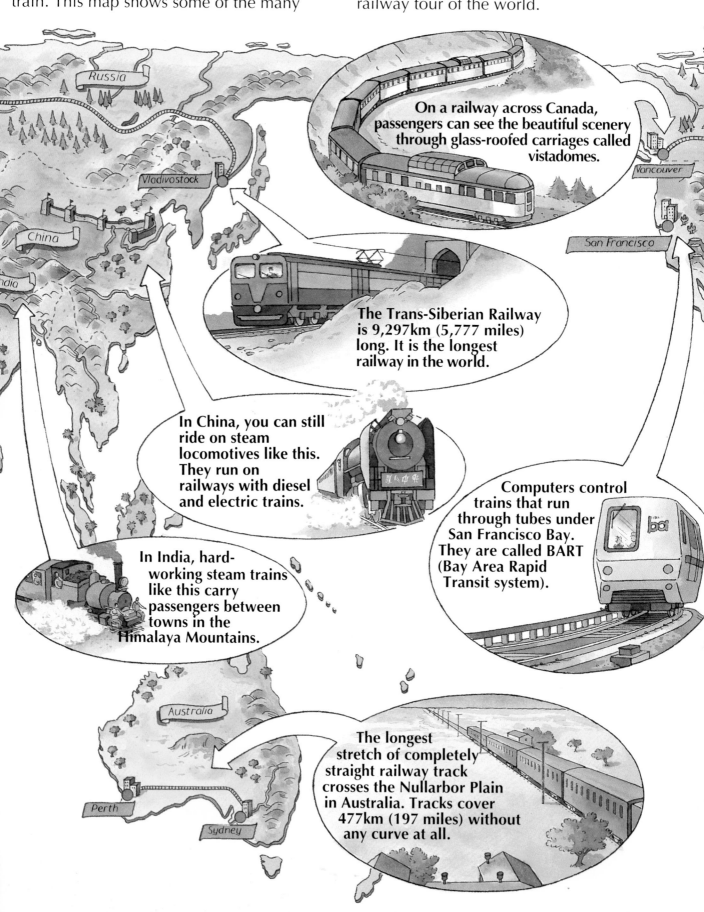

On a railway across Canada, passengers can see the beautiful scenery through glass-roofed carriages called vistadomes.

The Trans-Siberian Railway is 9,297km (5,777 miles) long. It is the longest railway in the world.

In China, you can still ride on steam locomotives like this. They run on railways with diesel and electric trains.

Computers control trains that run through tubes under San Francisco Bay. They are called BART (Bay Area Rapid Transit system).

In India, hard-working steam trains like this carry passengers between towns in the Himalaya Mountains.

The longest stretch of completely straight railway track crosses the Nullarbor Plain in Australia. Tracks cover 477km (197 miles) without any curve at all.

Russia
Vladivostock
China
India
Vancouver
San Francisco
Australia
Perth
Sydney

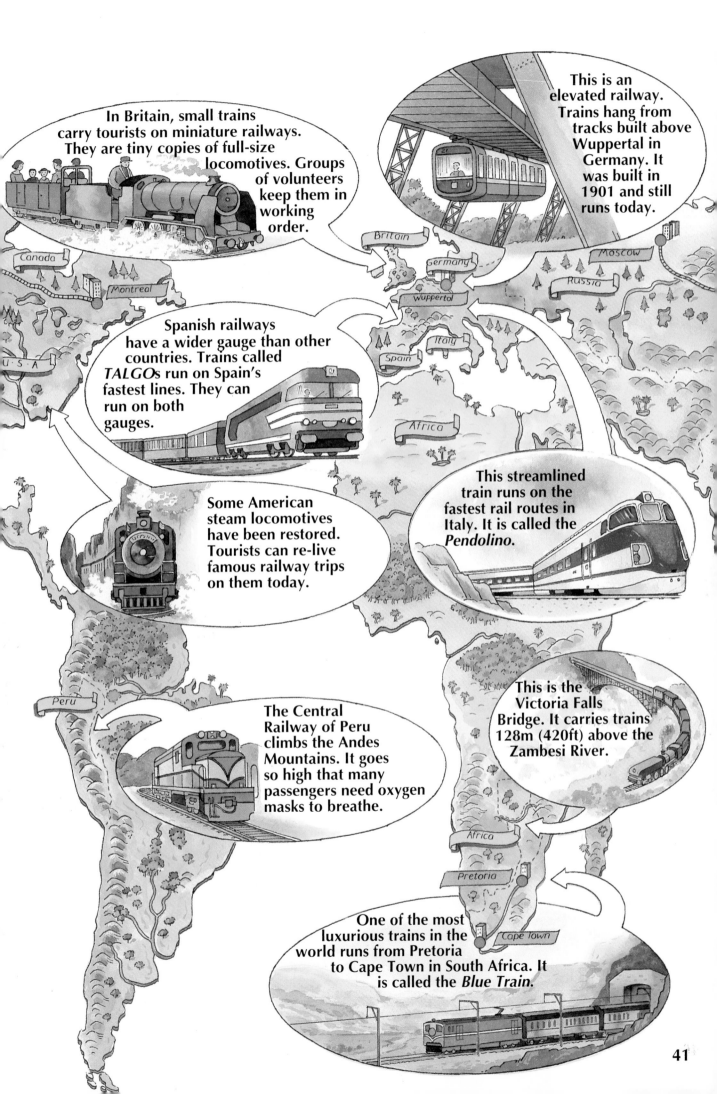

41

Trains and railways of the future

Today, railway engineers are trying out new sorts of trains that could run on the railways of the future. Here are some of the projects they are working on.

Trains under the sea

In 1994 the Channel Tunnel was opened between England and France. It is 50.5 km (31.5 miles) long, the longest undersea railway tunnel in the world.

Trains called shuttles carry cars, trucks and their passengers through the tunnel. The whole train journey lasts only 35 minutes.

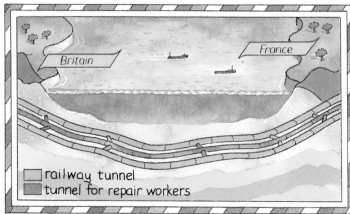

railway tunnel
tunnel for repair workers

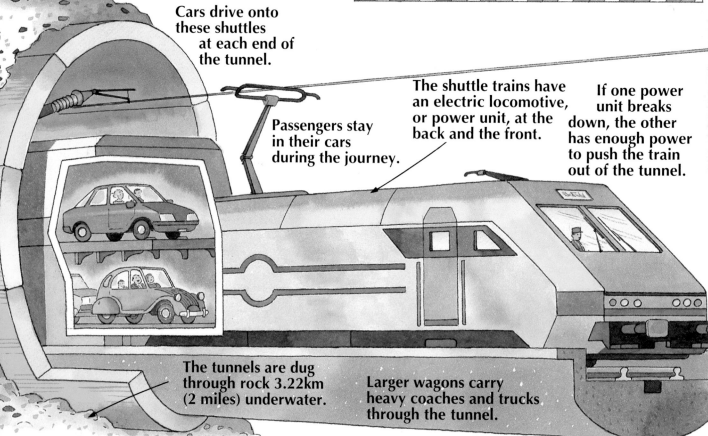

Cars drive onto these shuttles at each end of the tunnel.

Passengers stay in their cars during the journey.

The shuttle trains have an electric locomotive, or power unit, at the back and the front.

If one power unit breaks down, the other has enough power to push the train out of the tunnel.

The tunnels are dug through rock 3.22km (2 miles) underwater.

Larger wagons carry heavy coaches and trucks through the tunnel.

Driverless trains

In the future, trains may not need drivers. Computers will control them. Some experts think that computers will be safer drivers than humans and there will be fewer accidents on railways.

Driverless trains like this began work in part of London called Docklands in 1988. They are programmed by computer.

Passengers can sit at the front of the train to get the best view.

Maglev trains

Engineers in several countries are testing trains that run on magnetic power. They are called Maglev trains. Maglev trains have no wheels. They float above a magnetic track. They can go faster than any other type of train and make no noise or smoke at all.

What is magnetic power?

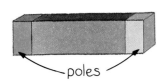

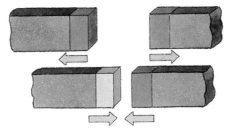

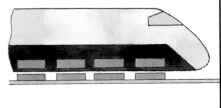

Magnets can make things move with an invisible power called magnetic force. It is strongest at the ends of the magnet, called the poles.

Every magnet has two types of pole. Two of the same type push away from each other. Two different types pull together.

When the magnets on a Maglev train and its track are the same poles, they push against each other. This lifts the train up. A special motor pushes it forwards.

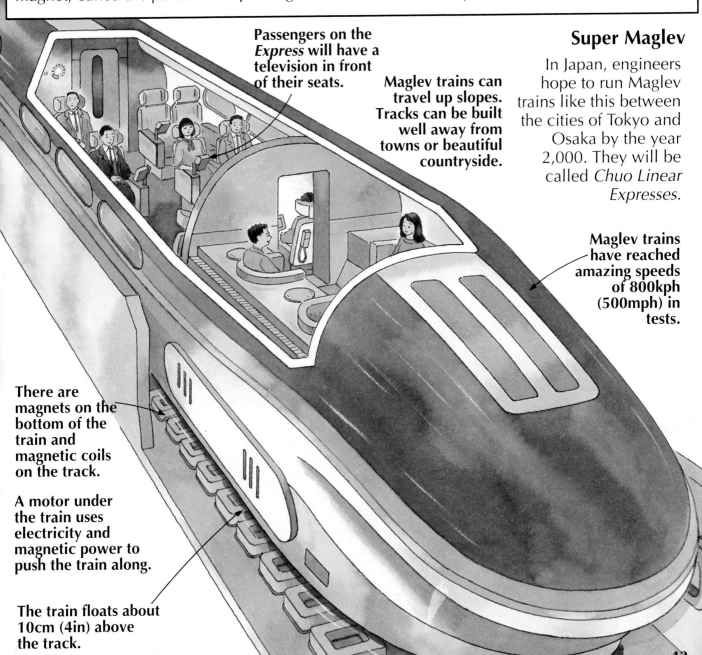

Passengers on the *Express* will have a television in front of their seats.

Maglev trains can travel up slopes. Tracks can be built well away from towns or beautiful countryside.

Super Maglev

In Japan, engineers hope to run Maglev trains like this between the cities of Tokyo and Osaka by the year 2,000. They will be called *Chuo Linear Expresses*.

Maglev trains have reached amazing speeds of 800kph (500mph) in tests.

There are magnets on the bottom of the train and magnetic coils on the track.

A motor under the train uses electricity and magnetic power to push the train along.

The train floats about 10cm (4in) above the track.

Time Line

Ancient Romans drove carts in ruts 2,000 years ago

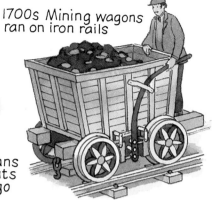

1700s Mining wagons ran on iron rails

1804 Richard Trevithick's steam locomotive pulled a heavy load at a mine in Wales

Coloured flags used as signals on railways to stop trains crashing into each other

1830s Railway-building starts all over Europe, North America and Russia

1831 The four-wheel bogie invented in North America

1859 George Pullman built his first luxury passenger carriage in America

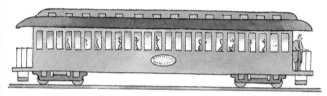

1863 First underground railway opened in London. Steam locomotives ran on it

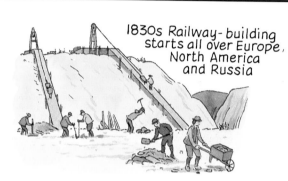

1869 Two railroads met at Promontory Point to carry trains across North America

1890 First electric underground train ran in London. Nicknamed the 'Padded Cell' as it had small windows

1883 First Orient Express ran from Paris to Istanbul in Turkey

1892 Sir Rudolf Diesel invented the diesel engine

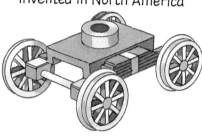

1950s Electric railways built in Europe after the second World War (1939-1945)

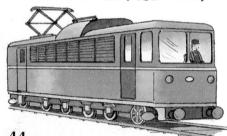

1964 Electric 'Bullet' trains started running in Japan

1981 TGV train began running on French railways. It reached 250 kph (160 mph)

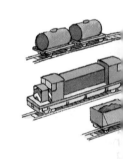
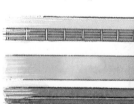

1810-15 Engineers found wheels with rims called flanges stayed on rails best

1825 First passenger railway in the world opened between Stockton and Darlington in England

1829 Rainhill Trials held to find the best sort of locomotive. The Stephensons' Rocket wins

1839 First railway timetable, called Bradshaw's, published

1841 Thomas Cook runs the first railway excursion

1840s Wooden semaphore railway signals used for the first time. Signalboxes appear on busy railways

1871 The first tunnel through the Alps Mountains finished. Three more were built in the next 30 years

1879 Siemens showed his electric locomotive at the Berlin exhibition

Early 1900's marshalling yards used to sort freight wagons into freight trains

1938 'Mallard' set the world speed record for a steam locomotive, reaching 203 kph (126 mph)

1939 Diesel train 'Flying Hamburger' reached 214 kph (133.5 mph)

1984 Small Maglev train started work at Birmingham Airport, England

1987 Work began on railway link between Britain and France, the Channel Tunnel

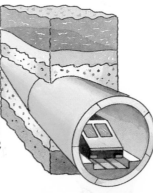

1990 TGV Atlantic reaches 515 kph (320 mph). It is the fastest passenger train yet

Glossary

Axle: the metal bar joining a pair of wheels together.

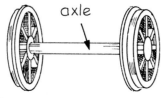

Ballast: small stones laid under and next to a railway track to make its base.

Blastpipe: pipe which takes exhaust steam from the **cylinders** of a steam **locomotive** up the **chimney**.

Boiler: metal drum on a steam **locomotive** in which water is turned into steam.

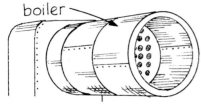

Bogie: trolley with four or six small wheels which is fixed to one end of a **locomotive**, **carriage** or **wagon**.

Carriage: part of a train in which passengers travel.

Carrying wheel: a wheel which helps guide a **locomotive** and bear its load. It is not linked to the **pistons** with **connecting rods**.

Chimney: tube where steam or smoke comes out of a **locomotive**. Sometimes called the **smokestack**.

Cab: part of a **locomotive** where the driver sits and controls the train.

Commuter: a person who lives in one place and travels to another to work.

Compartment: a separate small room inside a railway **carriage**.

Connecting rods: metal rods which join the **pistons** to the wheels of a **locomotive**.

Cowcatcher: metal cage fitted to the front of a **locomotive** to push animals off the track.

Coupling rods: metal rods which link pairs of wheels together on a **locomotive** so that they turn around at the same time.

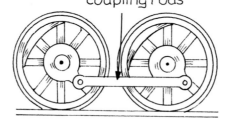

Cutting: a trough dug through a hill or under a street for the railway to be built in.

Cylinder: metal tube into which steam or hot gas is pushed to move the **pistons** backwards and forwards.

Driving wheel: main wheel, driven around by **connecting rods** from the engine.

Elevated railway: railway which runs on tracks built above the ground.

Embankment: valley or dip filled-in to make flat ground for railway tracks.

Excursion: organised trip offering tickets to passengers at less than their normal price.

Exhaust: steam from the **boiler** after it has gone through the **cylinders**.

Firebox: metal box behind the **boiler** in which the fire burns on a steam **locomotive**.

Fireman: person who shovels coal into a steam **locomotive's firebox** and checks the water in its **boiler**.

Flange: rim on one side of a wheel to keep it on the rail.

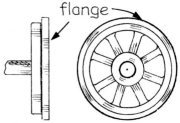

Footplate: area behind the **firebox** of a steam **locomotive** where the driver and fireman stand to control it.

Freight: goods or cargo

Funicular: a railway up a steep slope with two cars hauled by metal cables.

Galley: kitchen on a train.

Gauge: distance between two **rails** of a railway track.

Gradient: a slope or uphill piece of road or railway track. Trains cannot climb steep gradients.

Locomotive: an engine which makes it own power to move.

Maglev: short for 'magnetic levitation'. This means 'lifting up by the power of **magnetism**'.

Magnetism: power produced by magnets. Magnets can push things away or pull things towards them with it.

Marshalling yard: place where **freight** wagons are sorted into **freight** trains.

Navvy: Short for 'navigator'. A person who built the early railways.

Pantograph: wire frame on top of electric trains which picks up electricity from cables above the track.

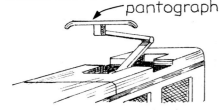
pantograph

Piston: metal plug which slides backwards and forwards inside a **cylinder** as steam pushes against it.

Power unit: another name for an electric **locomotive**.

Power box: **signal box** controlling a large area of the track using an electric diagram of that track.

Rack and pinion: toothed track (rack) and toothed wheels (pinions) which pull trains up mountains.

rack and pinion

Rail: strip of metal which a train's wheels run on. Usually made of steel.

Retarder: machine inside railway tracks which slows down moving **freight** wagons in a **marshalling yard**.

Safety valve: part on top of a steam **locomotive** where steam comes out if pressure inside the **boiler** is too high.

safety valve

Saloon: railway **carriage** built for passengers to relax in.

Semaphore: type of railway **signal**, made of wooden or metal strips which can move into different positions.

Shunting: pushing **carriages** or **wagons** to sort them into the right order to make a train.

Signal: a sign which tells a train driver what to do. There are several different sorts.

Siding: piece of track where trains are parked between journeys or sorted into complete trains.

Sleeper: wooden or concrete strip which the **rails** of a railway are laid on.

Smokebox: part of a steam **locomotive** where steam and smoke collect before going up the **chimney**.

Smokestack: wide steam **locomotive chimney** which catches burning sparks.

Streamlined: built with a smooth shape to go faster.

Telegraph: machine for sending messages down an electric wire to another telegraph machine.

Tender: **wagon** behind a steam **locomotive** which carries the fuel and water.

tender

Traction motor: motor which makes wheels turn when supplied with electric power.

Trestle bridge: bridge built of logs or planks of wood resting on each other.

Valve: hole which lets steam, water or gas in and out.

Viaduct: bridge taking a railway or road across a deep or wide valley.

Vistadome: railway **carriage** with a glass roof.

Wagon: a railway **carriage** built to carry **freight**.

Weatherboard: metal panel on early steam **locomotives** to protect the crew.

weatherboard

Wheel arrangement: the number and order of a **locomotive's driving** and **carrying wheels**.

Index

First published in 1991 by Usborne Publishing Ltd, Usborne House, 83-85 Saffron Hill, London, EC1 8RT London.

Printed in Hong Kong / China
The name Usborne and the device 🎈 are trademarks of Usborne Publishing Ltd.